EXODUS
ON KODI

Step by step instructions on
how to install exodus on Kodi
(With Detailed screenshots)

SEAN WILLIAMS

Contents

Kodi Exodus Latest Version (XvBMC Repository)

Copyright Page

PART 1

WHAT IS KODI

Kodi is a user free software developed by the XBMC Foundation, a non-profit technology consortium. Kodi gives you the ability to stream anything online. Kodi is available on all device namely Android, Windows, Amazon Fire TV/Stick, Mac OS, XBOX, Linux and Raspberry Pi. It an entertainment software that allows you to view TV Shows and Movies with Kodi addons, but for you to enjoy these services you need to have Kodi VPN.

Officially Kodi was launched in 2002 as Xbox Media Player (XBMP) after sometimes it was changed to Xbox Media Center (XBMC). In august 2014, due to limitation the software may face using Xbox, the software company decided to change its name to Kodi and equally add more features.

Furthermore, Kodi add-ons allow the software to stream anything, there are developers that develop add-ons for Kodi, these services are sometimes free and costly but making use of it will make a difference to its users.

Is Kodi Legal?

Yes, Kodi is legal only when you use its official add-ons. Kodi have an inbuilt repository when you install the app for its users, any add-ons not recommended by Kodi is built by third-party.

Kodi Third-Party Add-ons

Add-Ons developed by third-party are not associated with Kodi. These add-ons bring you free movies, TV Shows, Live TV, etc., all this are source from free streaming websites on the internet and Torrents.

Is Kodi Illegal?

When you are watching copyright materials for free on Kodi, but not all copyright material is illegal, the reasons being this, some add-ons tools help stop buffering issues in Kodi and also help to clear Kodi cache

Add-ons that generate free movies and TV shows from torrents and from the internet are illegal, Kodi have taken steps in recent years to crackdown third-party developers

Kodi is illegal when you must have installed add-ons that is not directly from Kodi because these add-ons allow you to watch free content on the internet on Kodi, then that when Kodi is illegal

Kodi VPN

Kodi VPN will enable you to enjoy unlimited services on Kodi without been restricted, it will kind of mask the IP you are using with a foreign IP USA, UK, Canada, etc. to mention few where the channel you are using is available.

You will be able to view your favorite channels without being restricted anywhere in the world

The underlisted VPN is suggested by User reviews and Kodi fans, due to their P2P supported servers and optimized streaming for high-speed video quality and online music streaming.

1 PureVPN

2 NordVPN

3 IvacyVPN

4 PrivateVPN

5 ExpressVPN

Note- this listed VPN are offered to you based on what its users review

PUREVPN

PureVPN is arguably one of the best VPN dues to its wide range servers, Kodi can be accessed by using one of its servers, the software will help solve issues like buffering delays, IP leakage and you can access blocked add-ons instantly.

One of the key reason I recommend the VPN is because it is available on VPN manager for OpenVPN add-ons. You can setup PureVPN on Kodi directly to enjoy online content and also PureVPN developed an app for android users and can be installed easily on your device

How to Download PureVPN Kodi Add-on (Method 1)

Step 1: install the PureVPN Repository Zip File

Step 2: Launch Kodi

> Tap on Add-ons section on your left

Step 3: Tap on the Box-icon

> Choose Install from Zip File

Step 4: When the box appears, search for the downloaded Zip File and Upload

> Wait till it successfully install PureVPN Kodi add-on

Step 5: Return to Kodi Homepage

> Click on Add-ons, Then Program Add-ons

> Choose PureVPN

Step 6: Under the PureVPN Kodi add-on Click on Add-ons Settings option.

Step 7: Enter Username and Password

> press OK

> Now stream Kodi safely!

How to Setup PureVPN Kodi Addon (Method-2)

PureVPN also offers its own exclusive add-on for Kodi.

All you need to do is follow these steps to setup the VPN on Kodi:

Start Kodi and go to Settings

>Then select File Manager

> Click Add Source, when a box appears, select 'None'

> Paste the URL: https://www.purevpn.com/Kodi-repo/

>Then select Done

> Name the addon (Kodi-repo) or any name of your choice

> Click Done

> Click Ok

Return to Kodi home screen on your device

Select on Add-ons

> then Add-on Browser (the package box icon at the top left corner)

> Install from zip file

> Kodi-repo

> purevpn.monitor-1.2.5.zip

Wait for the repository to install

Return to Install from repository

> Kodi-repo

> Program add-ons

> PureVPN Monitor Open VPN

After the downloaded add-on is installed, Locate Program Add-ons

> PureVPN Monitor OpenVPN

> Add-on Settings

A box will show up, enter your PureVPN credentials (username and password), Tap on change the server location, Click on Display VPN status and choose the server location of your choice and it will connect automatically

Congratulations, you are not ready to use PureVPN Kodi add-on

PART 2

Steps for Downloading Kodi

The first step is to install Kodi from the play store or from the Kodi website

Kodi play store

Kodi website

Configure Settings Before Installing Exodus on Kodi

Kodi restrict add-ons coming from unknown developers, so before you install Exodus you need to allow the option in setting

Go to Kodi homepage, click Settings

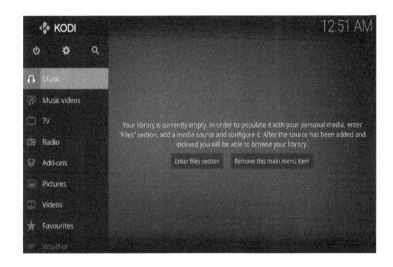

> System settings

Select Add-ons, tap Unknown sources, then
confirm by clicking 'Yes'.

PART 3

Exodus on Kodi: Installation procedure

Ways to install exodus on Kodi 17.6

Install Exodus Kodi 17.6 with Lazy Kodi Repository

Step 1: Enter Kodi homepage > click on Settings icon at the top

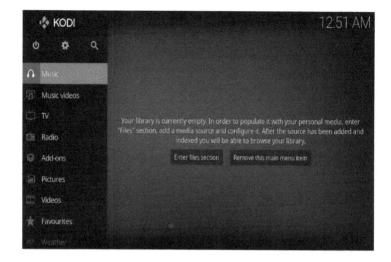

> Click on File Manager

Step 2: click on Add Source twice >

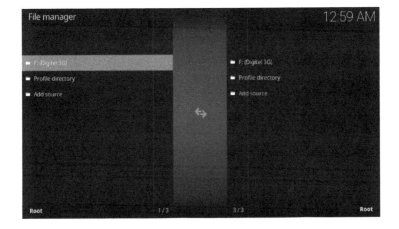

> select 'None' when the box shows up

Step 3: a box will pop up when you select 'None' then, Paste the URL
http://lazykodi.com/ > Press OK

> Save repository i.e.my Lazy Kodi >then Press OK

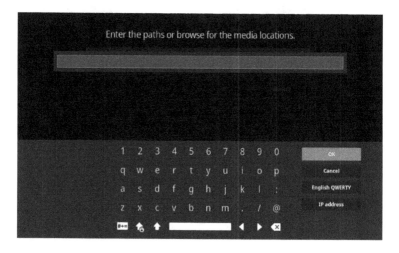

Step 4: Return to Kodi Home > Select Add-ons menu

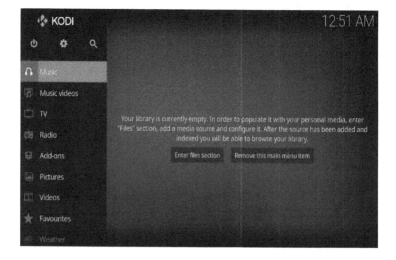

> Tap on Box-shaped icon,

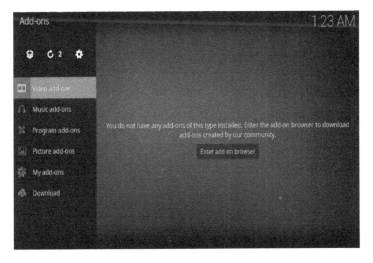

Step 5: Click on Install from Zip File

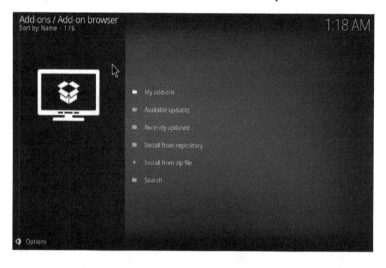

Quick reminder- For those new to Kodi

When you click on install from zip file, some security notification will appear

When you see this on your screen, all you need to do is to enable by clicking the setting option, then click on the unknown source option to enable

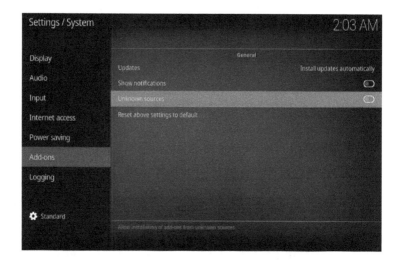

> When the box opens click on Lazy Kodi

Step 6: choose Repositories section

> Then tap on Adroidaba

> Click onto Repository

> Now select repository.kodil-1.4.zip

> wait for the repository to install

Step 7: Go to Install from Repository option

> click on Kodil Repository from the list

> Return to Video Add-ons > Find Exodus

> click Install

How to Install Exodus Kodi 17.6 with Kodi Bae Repository

Step 1: Download Kodi Bae Repository Zip File

Step 2: Open Kodi

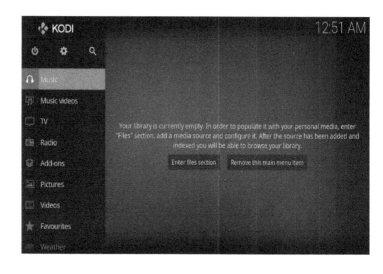

> find Add-ons section

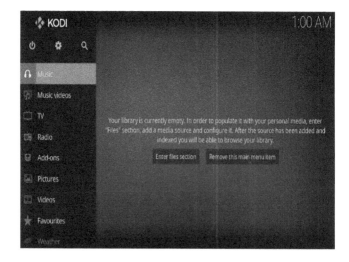

> Select on Box-icon

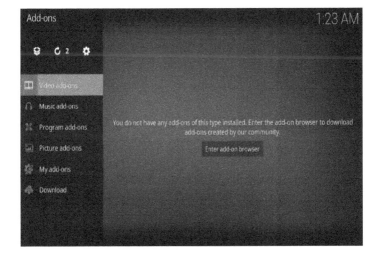

Step 3: Choose Install from Zip File

> Upload the downloaded Kodi Bae Zip File

> When begin to upload the file it will take some time to install

Step 4: Now the Exodus add-on is installed. To view the add-on, Return to Kodi Home

> Tap Add-ons section > Video Add-ons > Exodus > Enjoy!

Kodi Exodus Latest Version (XvBMC Repository)

This new repository hosts popular Kodi add-ons like Exodus, Covenant, Community Portal.

How to Install Exodus Kodi 17.6 with XvBMC Repository

Step 1: Go to Kodi Krypton

> Click on Settings gear-icon on top

> Then click on File Manager

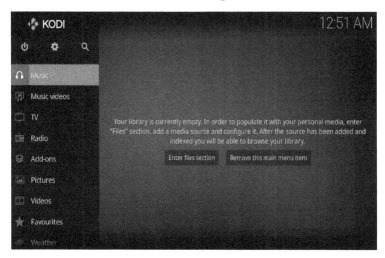

> Select File Manager

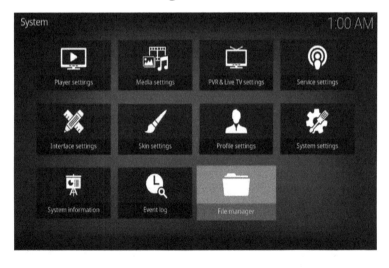

Step 2: Go down and click on Add Source
twice > A box appears, click on 'None'

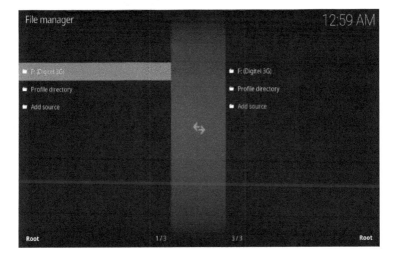

Step 3: Paste the URL
http://archive.org/download/repository.xv
bmc/ > select OK

> Name the media source i.e. With any
name of your choice> Press OK

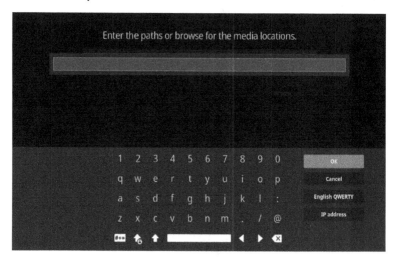

Step 4: Return to Kodi Main Menu

> Then select Add-ons

> Box icon on top

Step 5: Select Install from Zip File

> immediately the box appears, click on XvBMC

> Then select repository.xvbmc-4.20.zip

> Wait for the installation to complete

Step 6: tap on Install from Zip File

> Then choose XvBMC (Add-ons) Repository

Step 7: select Add-on Repository present at the top of the list

> Then select tknorris Release Repository
> select Install

Step 8: Go back two spaces by pressing on 'Backspace'

> Then choose tknorris Release Repository

Step 9: Go to Video Add-ons

> Now find and select Exodus

> Click Install

Copyright

www.ingramcontent.com/pod-product-compliance
Lightning Source LLC
Chambersburg PA
CBHW070905070326
40690CB00009B/2006